Impressum
Verlag: BABADADA GmbH, Nedderfeld 112 , 22529 Hamburg
Geschäftsführer / Verlagsleitung: Harald Hof
Druck: Books on Demand GmbH, In de Tarpen 42, 22848 Norderstedt

Imprint
Publisher: BABADADA GmbH, Nedderfeld 112 , 22529 Hamburg, Germany
Managing Director / Publishing direction: Harald Hof
Print: Books on Demand GmbH, In de Tarpen 42, 22848 Norderstedt

school

المدرسة

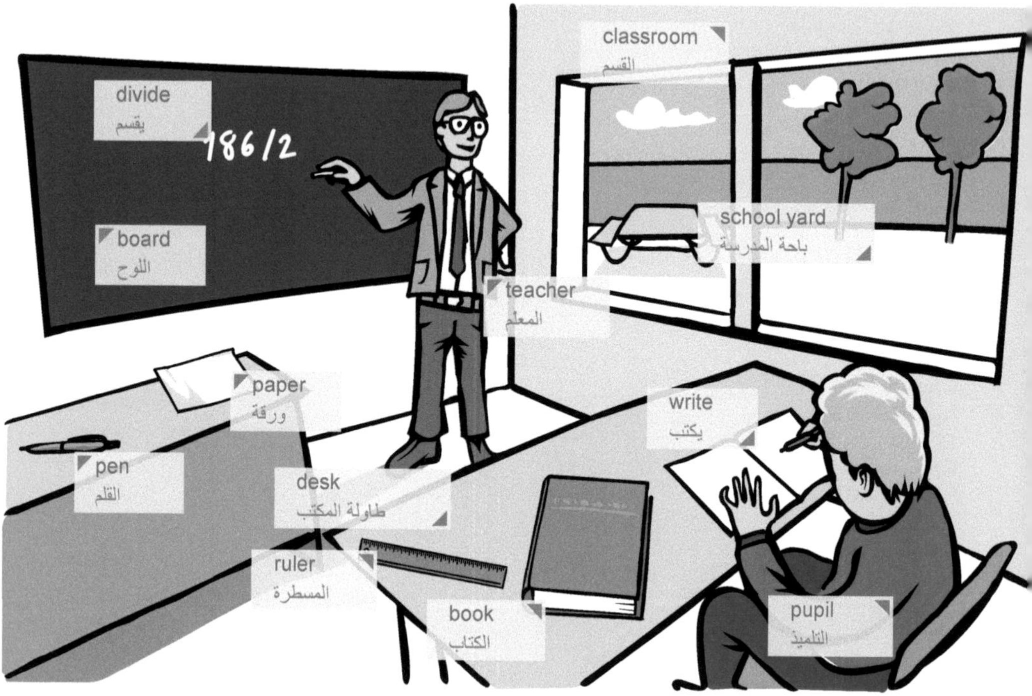
classroom
القسم
divide
يقسم
186/2
board
اللوح
school yard
باحة المدرسة
teacher
المعلم
paper
ورقة
write
يكتب
pen
القلم
desk
طاولة المكتب
ruler
المسطرة
book
الكتاب
pupil
التلميذ

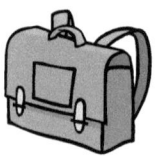

satchel

الحقيبة المدرسية

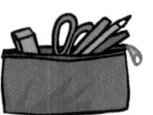

pencil case

المقلمة

pencil

قلم الرصاص

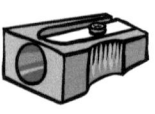

pencil sharpener

البرّاية

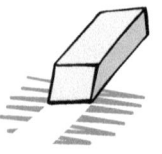

rubber

الممحاة

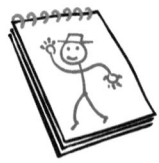

drawing pad

دفتر الرسم

drawing

الرسمة

paintbrush

الفرشاة

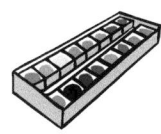

paint box

علبة التلوين

scissors

المقص

glue

المادة اللاصقة

exercise book

دفتر التمارين

homework

الواجب المدرسي

number

الرقم

add

يجمع

subtract

يطرح

multiply

يضرب

calculate

يحسب

letter

الحرف

alphabet

الأبجدية

word

كلمة

text

النص

read

يقرأ

chalk

الطبشور

lesson

الحصة

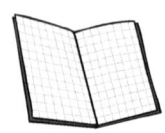

register

دفتر الدوام المدرسي

examination

الامتحان

certificate

شهادة

school uniform

اللباس المدرسي

education

التعليم

encyclopedia

الموسوعة

university

الجامعة

microscope

المجهر

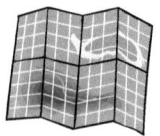

map

الخريطة

waste-paper basket

قماما

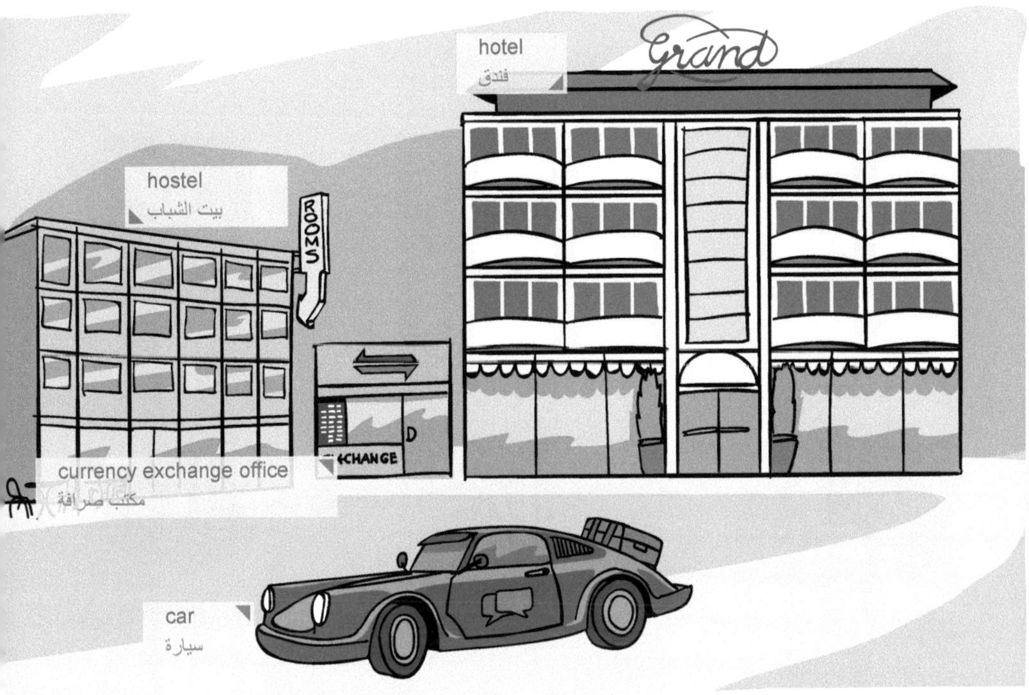
hotel
فندق
Grand
hostel
بيت الشباب
ROOMS
EXCHANGE
currency exchange office
مكتب صرافة
car
سيارة

language
اللغة

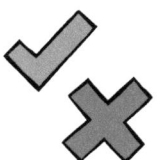

yes / no
نعم / لا

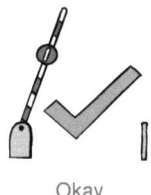

Okay
حسناً

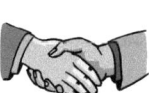

hello
مرحباً

translator
مترجم

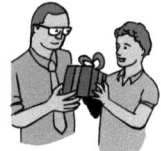

Thank you
شكراً

how much is...?

كم ثمن ... ؟

I don´t get it

لا أفهم

problem

مشكلة

Good evening!

مساء الخير

Good morning!

صباح الخير!

Good night!

ليلة سعيدة

goodbye

إلى اللقاء

direction

اتجاه

luggage

أمتعة السفر

bag

حقيبة

backpack

حقيبة ظهر

guest

ضيف

room

غرفة

sleeping bag

كيس للنوم

tent

خيمة

tourist information

استعلامات سياحية

beach

شاطئ

credit card

بطاقة ائتمان

breakfast

إفطار

lunch

طعام الغذاء

dinner

العشاء

Ticket

بطاقة سفر

elevator

مصعد

stamp

طابع بريدي

border

حدود

customs

الجمارك

embassy

سفارة

visa

تأشيرة

passport

جواز سفر

transport
نقل

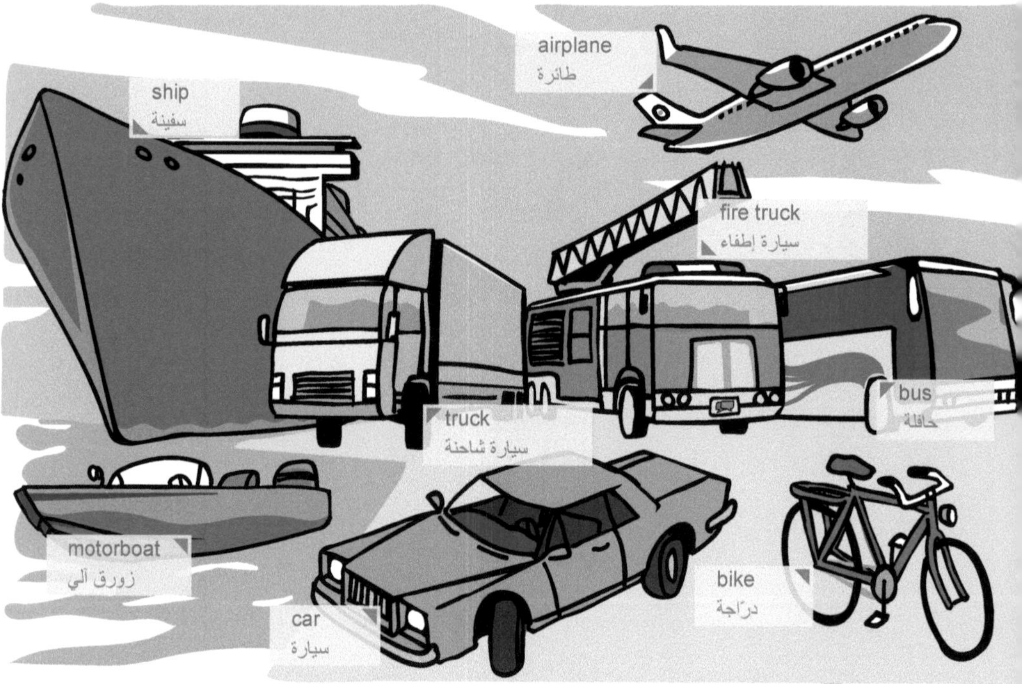

airplane
طائرة
ship
سفينة
fire truck
سيارة إطفاء
bus
حافلة
truck
سيارة شاحنة
motorboat
زورق آلي
bike
درّاجة
car
سيارة

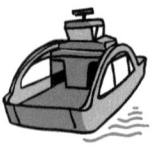

ferry

عبارة

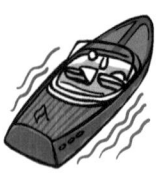

boat

قارب

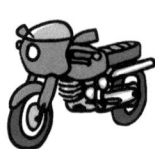

motorbike

دراجة نارية

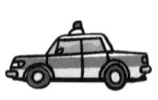

police car

سيارة شرطة

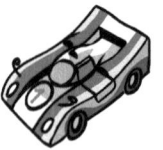

racing car

سيارة سباق

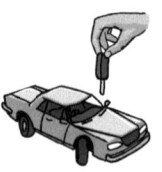

rental car

سيارة مستأجرة

car sharing

أسلوب تشاركي في استئجار السيارات

tow truck

سيارة للجر

garbage truck

سيارة نقل القمامة

engine

محرك

fuel

وقود

fuel station

محطة وقود

traffic sign

إشارة مرور

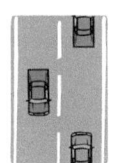

traffic

حركة السير

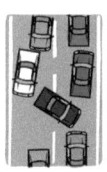

traffic jam

ازدحام سير

parking lot

موقف سيارات

train station

محطة قطار

tracks

سكك حديدية

train

قطار

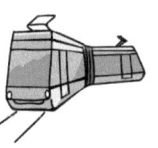

tram

ترام

wagon

عربة قطار

helicopter

طائرة مروحية

airport

مطار

tower

برج

passenger

مسافر

container

حاوية

carton

علبة كرتون

cart

عربة يد

basket

سلة

take off / land

يَقلع / يهبط

city

مدينة

village

قرية

city center

مركز المدينة

house

بيت

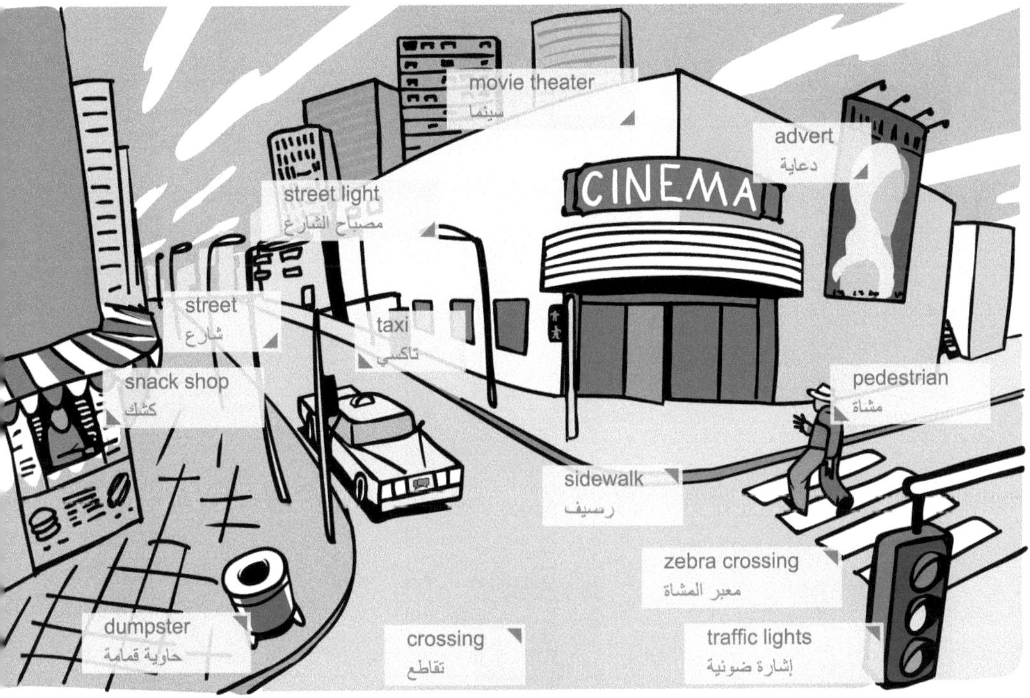

movie theater
سينما

advert
دعاية

CINEMA

street light
مصباح الشارع

street
شارع

taxi
تاكسي

pedestrian
مشاة

snack shop
كشك

sidewalk
رصيف

zebra crossing
معبر المشاة

dumpster
حاوية قمامة

crossing
تقاطع

traffic lights
إشارة ضوئية

hut

كوخ

apartment

شقة

train station

محطة قطار

city hall

دار البلدية

museum

متحف

school

المدرسة

university

الجامعة

bank

مصرف

hospital

المستشفى

hotel

فندق

pharmacy

صيدلية

office

مكتب

book shop

مكتبة

shop

متجر

flower shop

محل لبيع الزهور

supermarket

سوبرماركت

market

سوق

department store

متجر كبير

fishmonger's shop

تاجر السمك

mall

مركز تسوّق

harbor

ميناء

park

حديقة عامة

bench

مقعد

bridge

جسر

stairs

درج، سلم

subway

مترّو

tunnel

نفق

bus stop

موقف حافلات

bar

بار

restaurant

مطعم

postbox

صندوق البريد

street sign

لافتة باسم الشارع

parking meter

مقياس زمن الوقوف

zoo

حديقة حيوانات

swimming pool

مسبح

mosque

مسجد

farm

مزرعة

pollution

تلوث البيئة

cemetery

مقبرة

church

كنيسة

playground

ملعب الأطفال

temple

معبد

landscape

طبيعة ريفية

signpost
علامة إرشاد

path
طريق

meadow
مرج

stone
حجر

hiker
رحالة

tree
شجرة

river
نهر

grass
عشب

flower
زهرة

valley

وادٍ

hill

جبل

lake

بحيرة

forest

غابة

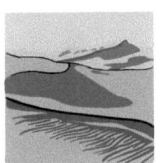

desert

صحراء

volcano

بركان

castle

قلعة

rainbow

قوس قزح

mushroom

فطر

palm tree

نخلة

mosquito

بعوض

fly

ذبابة

ant

نملة

bee

نحلة

spider

عنكبوت

beetle

خنفساء

frog

ضفدعة

squirrel

سنجاب

hedgehog

قنفذ

hare

أرنب

owl

بومة

bird

عصفور

swan

بجعة

boar

خنزير برّي

deer

غزال

moose

إلكة

dam

سد

wind turbine

دولاب الطاحونة الهوائية

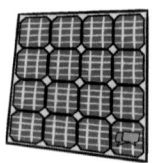

solar panel

خلية شمسية

climate

مناخ

restaurant
مطعم

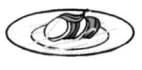

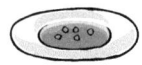

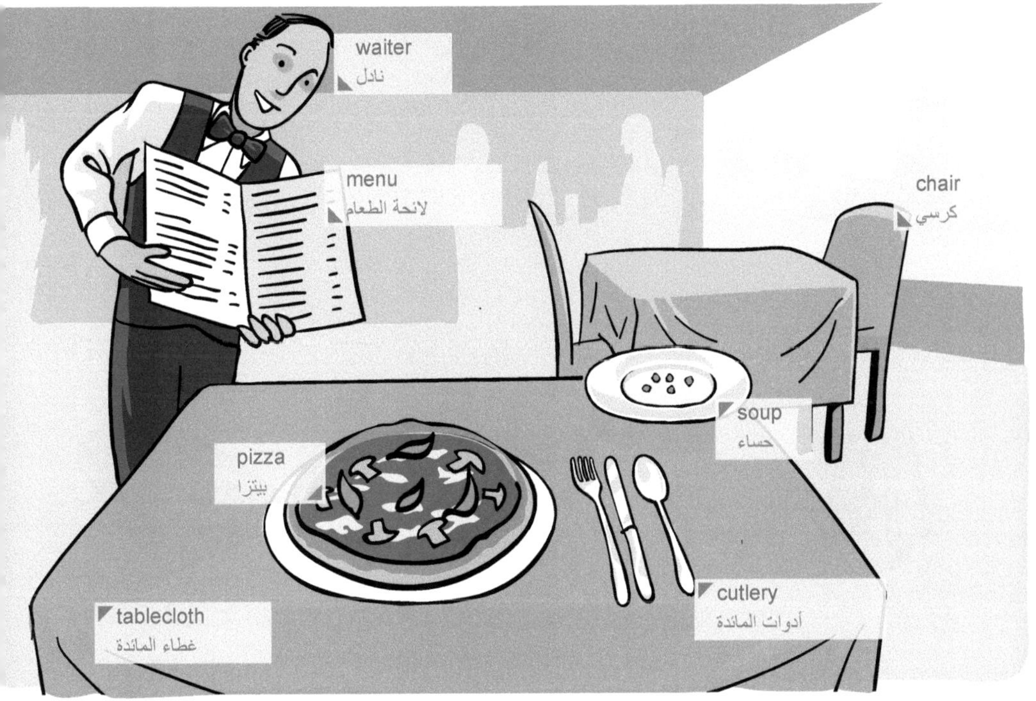
waiter
نادل
menu
لائحة الطعام
chair
كرسي
soup
حساء
pizza
بيتزا
cutlery
أدوات المائدة
tablecloth
غطاء المائدة

starter

مقبلات

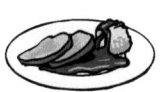

main course

الصحن الرئيسي

dessert

حلوى أو فاكهة بعد الطعام

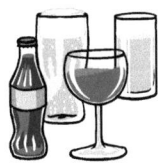

drinks

مشروبات

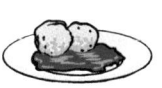

food

طعام

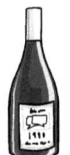

bottle

زجاجة

fast food

وجبات سريعة

street food

طعام الشارع

teapot

إبريق الشاي

sugar bowl

علبة السكر

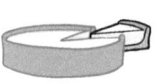

portion

حصّة

espresso machine

آلة الإسبريسو

high chair

كرسي عالٍ

bill

فاتورة

tray

صينية

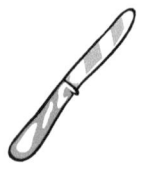

knife

سكين

fork

شوكة

spoon

ملعقة

teaspoon

ملعقة الشاي

serviette

منديل المائدة

glass

كأس

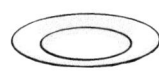

plate

صحن

soup plate

صحن الحساء

saucer

صحن الفنجان

sauce

صلصة

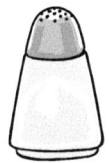

salt shaker

مملحة

pepper mill

مطحنة الفلفل

vinegar

خلّ

oil

زيت الطعام

spices

توابل

ketchup

كتشاب

mustard

خردل

mayonnaise

مايونيز

supermarket
سوبرماركت

special offer
عرض خاص
FOR
customer
زبون
dairy products
مشتقات الحليب
fruit
فواكه
shopping cart
عربة تسوّق

BUTCHERS

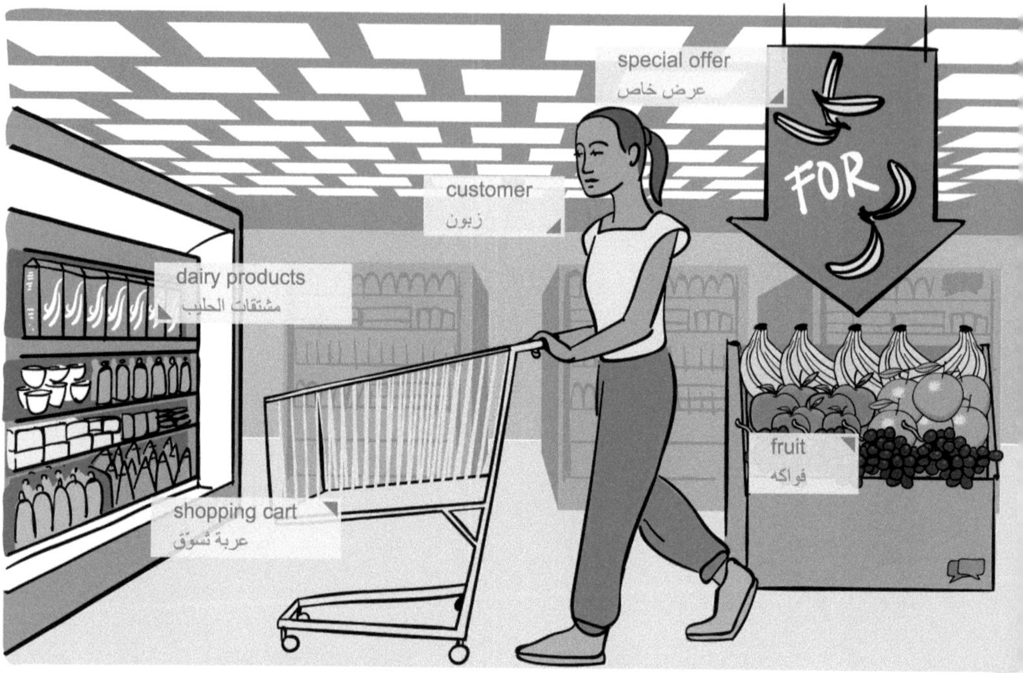

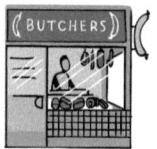

butcher's shop
جزّار

BAKERY

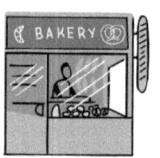

bakery
مخبز

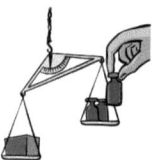

weigh
يزن

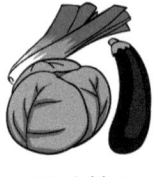

vegetables
خضار

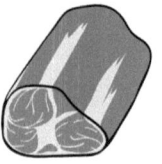

meat
لحم

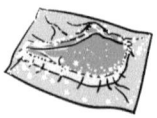

frozen food
المأكولات المجمّدة

cold cuts

مرتديلا أو جبن

canned food

معلّبات

detergent

مسحوق الغسيل

candy

حلويات

household products

المواد المنزلية

cleaning products

منظفات

sales representative

بائعة

cash register

صندوق الحساب

cashier

أمين صندوق

shopping list

قائمة المشتريات

opening hours

أوقات العمل

wallet

محفظة النقود

credit card

بطاقة ائتمان

bag

حقيبة

plastic bag

كيس بلاستيكي

water

ماء

juice

عصير

milk

حليب

coke

كولا

wine

نبيذ

beer

بيرة

alcohol

كحول

cocoa

كاكاو

tea

شاي

coffee

قهوة

espresso

قهوة إسبريسو

cappuccino

كابوتشينو

banana

موزة

apple

تفاح

orange

برتقال

melon

بطيخ

lemon

ليمون

carrot

جزرة

garlic

ثوم

bamboo

خيزران

onion

بصل

mushroom

فطر

nuts

لوزيات

noodles

شعيرية

spaghetti

سباغيتي

rice

أرزّ

salad

سلطة

fries

بطاطا مقلية

fried potatoes

بطاطا مقلية

pizza

بيتزا

hamburger

هامبورغر

sandwich

ساندويش

escalope

شريحة لحم مقلية

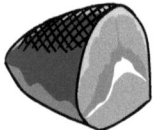

ham

لحم خنزير

salami

سلامي

sausage

سجق

chicken

دجاج

roast

لحم محمر

fish

سمك

porridge oats

دقيق الشوفان

muesli

موسلي

cornflakes

كورن فلكس

flour

طحين

croissant

كرواسان

bread roll

خبز صغير

bread

خبز

toast

خبز محمص

cookies

بسكويت

butter

زبدة

curd

لبن زبادي

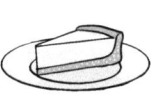

cake

كعكة

egg

بيضة

fried egg

بيض مقلي

cheese

جبنة

ice cream

مثلجات

sugar

سكر

honey

عسل

jelly

مربى الفاكهة

nougat cream

كريم النوغا

curry

الكاري

goat

ماعز

cow

بقرة

calf

عجل

pig

خنزير

piglet

خنزير صغير

bull

ثور

goose

إوزة

duck

بطة

chick

صوص

hen

دجاجة

cockerel

ديك

rat

جرذ

cat

قطة

mouse

فأر

ox

ثور

dog

كلب

dog house

كوخ الكلب

garden hose

خرطوم الحديقة

watering can

إبريق

scythe

منجل

plow

المحراث

sickle

منجل

hoe

معزقة

pitchfork

مذراة الزبل

axe

بلطة

pushcart

عربة يد

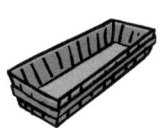

trough

معلف

milk can

صفيحة الحليب

sack

كيس

fence

سياج

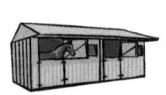

stable

اصطبل

greenhouse

دفيئة

soil

تربة

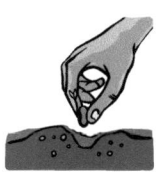

seed

بذور

fertilizer

سماد

combine harvester

حصادة دراسة

harvest

يحصد

harvest

محصول

yams

بطاطا يامس

wheat

قمح

soya

صويا

potato

بطاطا

corn

ذرة

rapeseed

سلجم

fruit tree

شجرة فاكهة

manioc

نبات منيهوت

grain

الحبوب

house
بيت

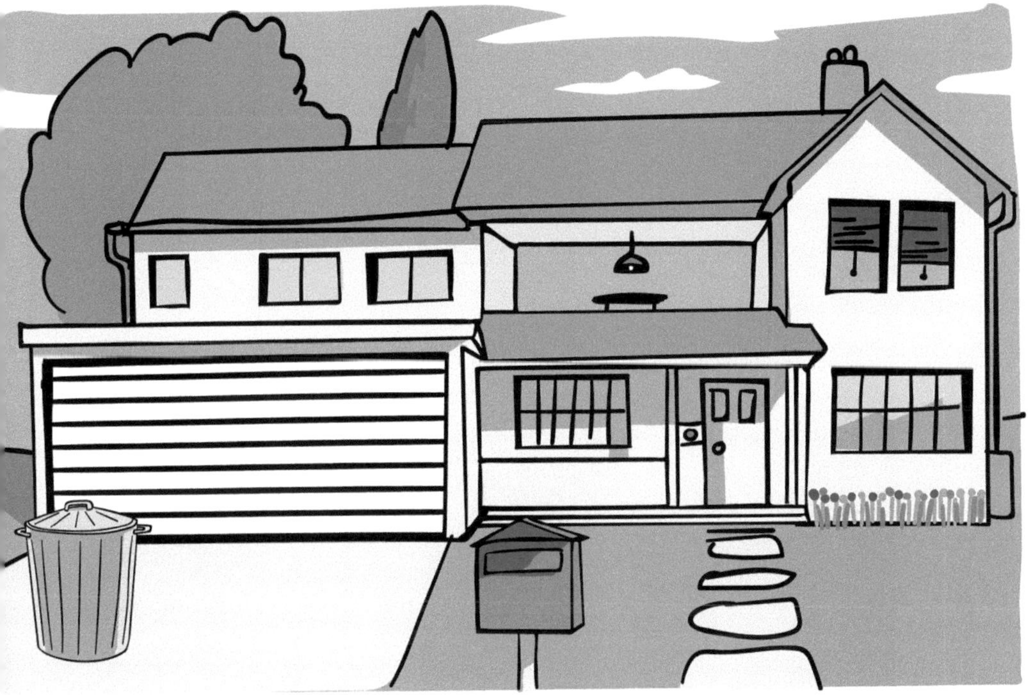

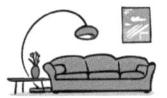

living room

غرفة جلوس

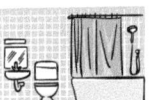

bathroom

الحمّام

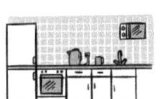

kitchen

مطبخ

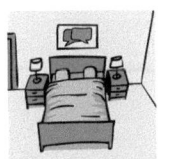

bedroom

غرفة النوم

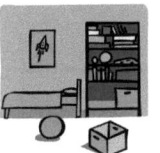

kids room

غرفة الأطفال

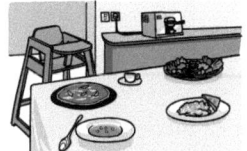

dining room

غرفة الطعام

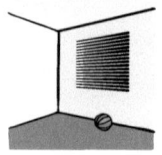

floor

أرضية

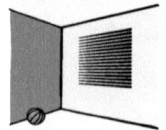

wall

حائط

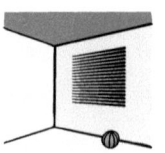

ceiling

سقف

cellar

قبو

sauna

ساونا

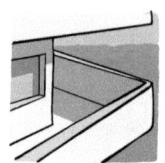

balcony

بلكون

terrace

شرفة

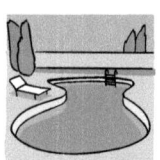

pool

مسبح

lawn mower

جزّازة العُشب

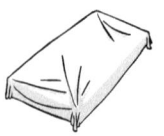

sheet

بياضات السرير

bedspread

بطانية

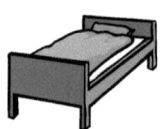

bed

سرير

broom

مكنسة

bucket

سطل

switch

مفتاح كهربائي

living room
غرفة جلوس

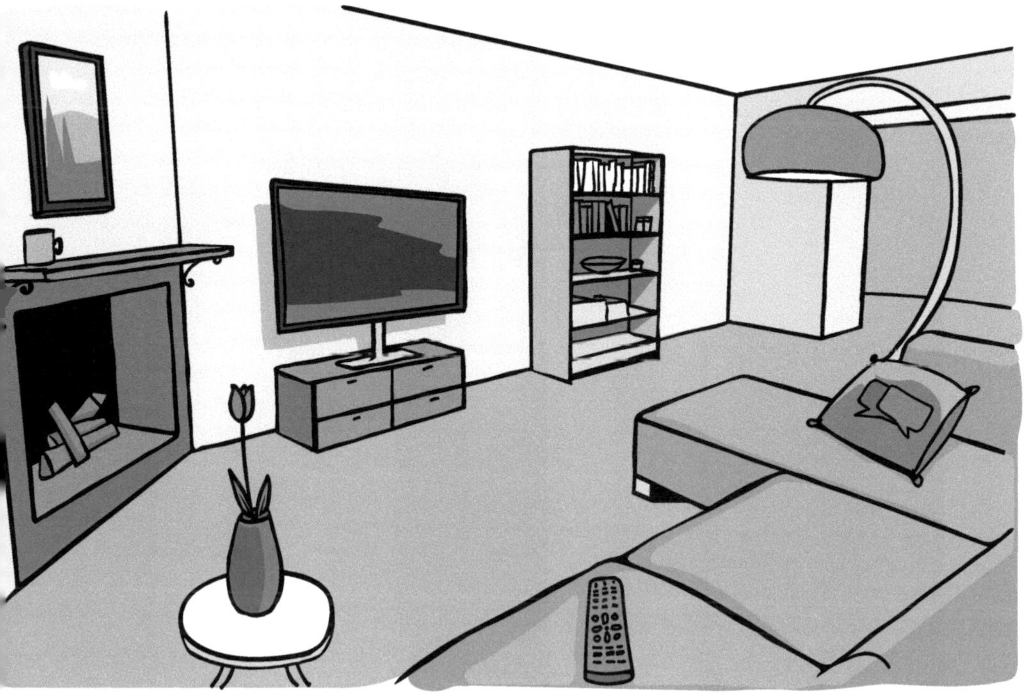

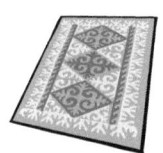

carpet

بساط

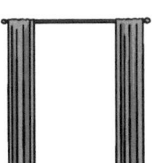

drape

ستارة

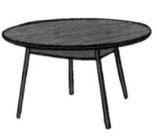

table

طاولة

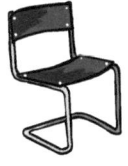

chair

كرسي

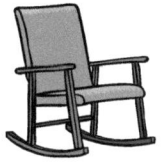

rocking chair

كرسي هزّاز

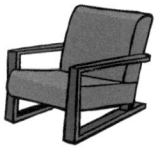

armchair

كرسي ذو ذراعين

book

الكتاب

blanket

بطانية

decoration

زخرفة

firewood

الحطب

film

فيلم

stereo system

تجهيزات ستيريو

key

مفتاح

newspaper

جريدة

painting

لوحة مرسومة

poster

مُلصق

radio

راديو

notebook

دفتر ملاحظات

vacuum cleaner

المكنسة الكهربائية

cactus

صبّار

candle

شمعة

kitchen
مطبخ

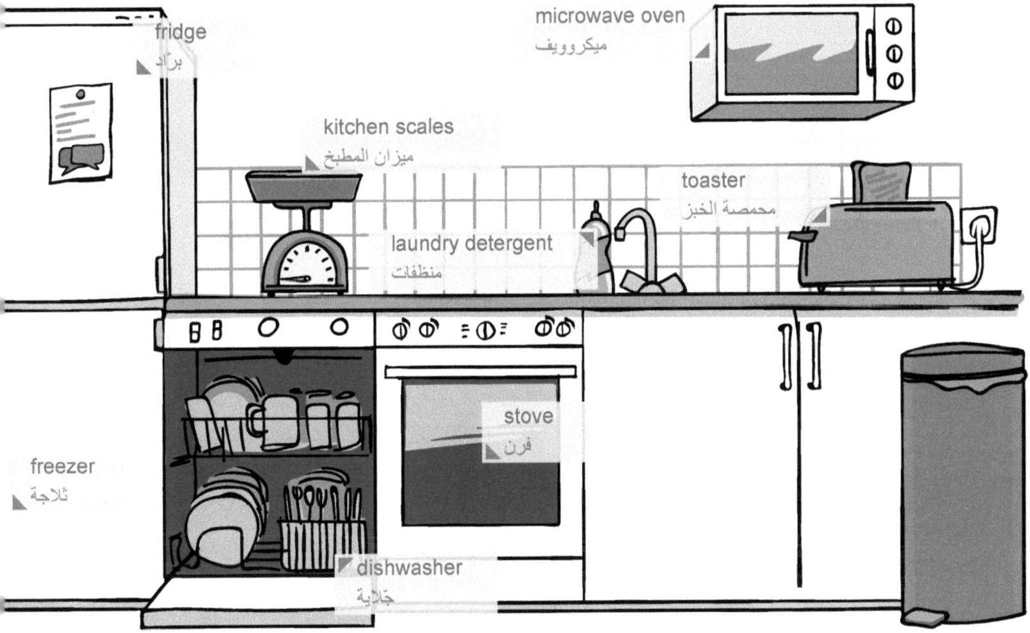
fridge
برّاد
microwave oven
ميكروويف
kitchen scales
ميزان المطبخ
toaster
محمصة الخبز
laundry detergent
منظفات
stove
فرن
freezer
ثلاجة
dishwasher
جلاية

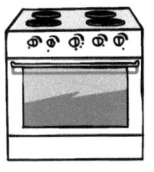

cooker
موقد

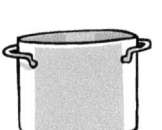

pot
قِدر

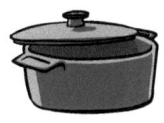

cast-iron pot
وعاء من الحديد

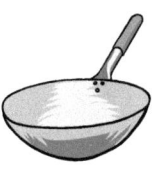

wok / kadai
قدر صيني

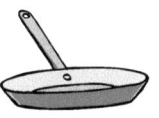

pan
مقلاة

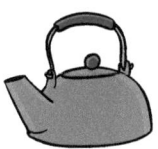

kettle
غلاية

steamer

قدر البخار

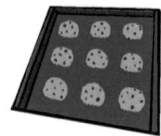

baking tray

صينية

crockery

أواني

mug

فنجان

bowl

صحن

chopsticks

عيدان الأكل

ladle

مغرفة

spatula

ملعقة منبسطة

whisk

خفاقة

strainer

مصفاة

sieve

مصفاة

grater

مبشرة

mortar

هاون

barbecue

شواء

fireplace

موقد

chopping board

لوح التقطيع

rolling pin

نشّابة

corkscrew

مفتاح الزجاجات

can

علبة

can opener

مفتاح العلب المعدنية

oven cloth

قماش الفرن

sink

مجلى

brush

فرشاة

sponge

إسفنج

blender

خلاط

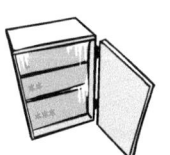

deep freezer

مجمّدة

baby bottle

زجاجة الطفل

tap

صنبور الماء

bathroom

الحمّام

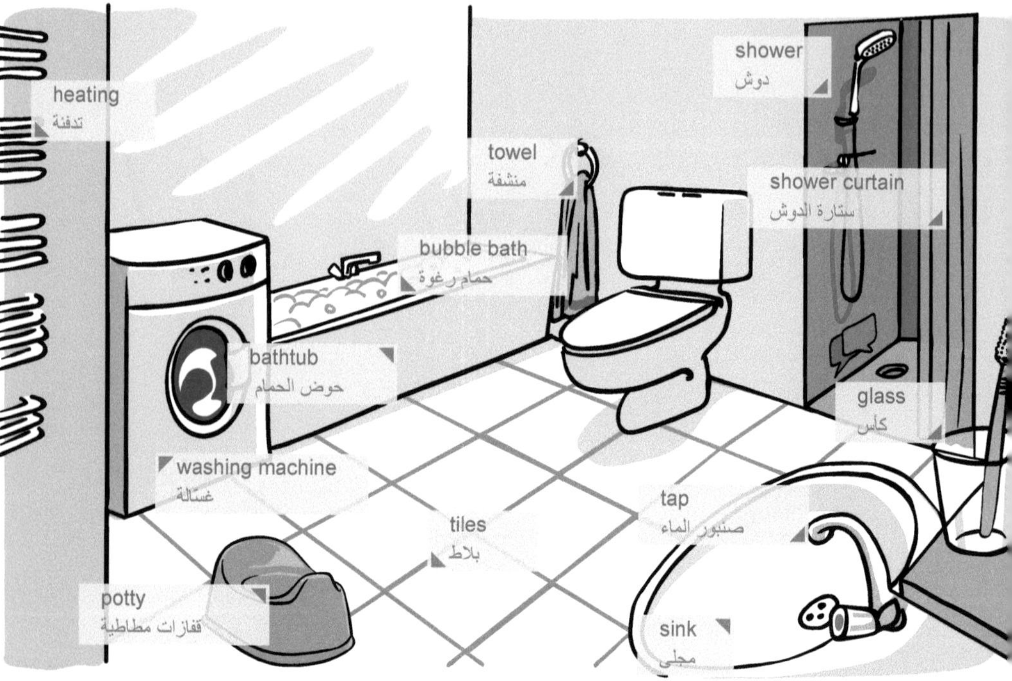

heating
تدفئة
shower
دوش
towel
منشفة
shower curtain
ستارة الدوش
bubble bath
حمام رغوة
bathtub
حوض الحمام
glass
كاس
washing machine
غسّالة
tap
صنبور الماء
tiles
بلاط
potty
قفازات مطاطية
sink
مجلى

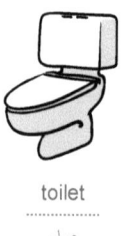

toilet

حمام

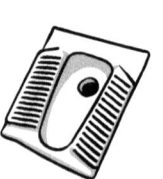

squat toilet

مرحاض القرفصاء

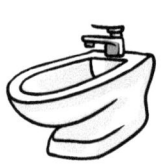

bidet

حوض التشطيف

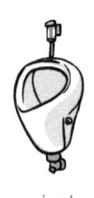

urinal

مبولة

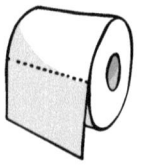

toilet paper

ورق المرحاض

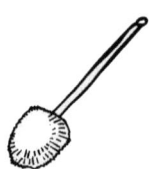

toilet brush

فرشاة الحمام

toothbrush

فرشاة الأسنان

toothpaste

معجون الأسنان

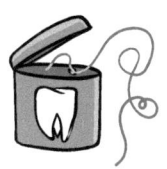

dental floss

خيط حرير لتنظيف الأسنان

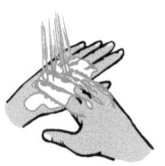

wash

يغسل

hand shower

رشّاش ماء يدوي

douche

شطّاف

basin

حوض الغسيل

back brush

فرشاة الظهر

soap

صابون

shower gel

جيل الدوش

shampoo

شامبو

flannel

ممسحة

drain

مصرف للماء

creme

مرهم

deodorant

مزيل الروائح

mirror

مرآة

hand mirror

مرآة يد

razor

موس حلاقة

shaving foam

رغوة الحلاقة

aftershave

كولونيا

comb

مشط

brush

فرشاة

hair-dryer

سشوار

hairspray

مثبت للشعر

makeup

ماكياج

lipstick

روج

nail varnish

طلاء أظافر

cotton wool

قطن

nail scissors

مقص أظافر

perfume

عطر

washbag

سلة الغسيل

stool

مقعد صغير

weighing scales

ميزان

bathrobe

معطف الحمام

rubber gloves

قفازات مطاطية

tampon

سدادة قطنية

sanitary towel

منشفة صحية

chemical toilet

تواليت كيميائية

kids room
غرفة الأطفال

alarm clock
منبه
cuddly toy
الحيوانات المحنطة
toy car
سيارة لعبة
rattle
خشخشة
doll's house
بيت الدمى
present
هدية

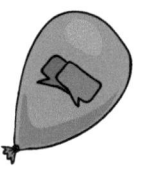

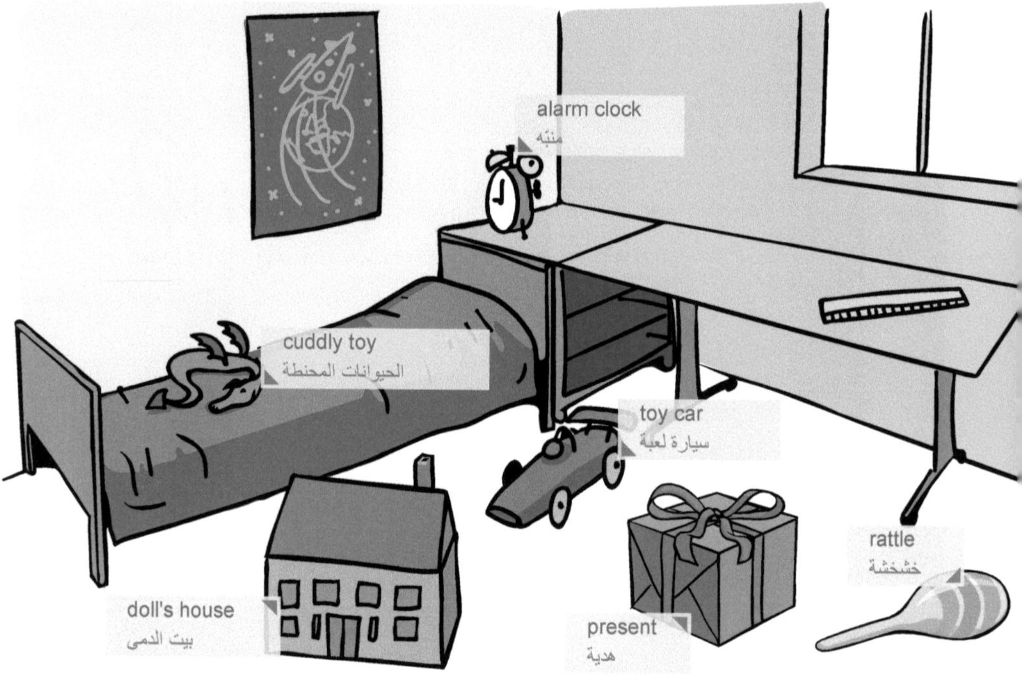

balloon
بالون

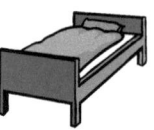

bed
سرير

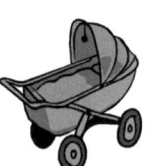

stroller
عربة الأطفال

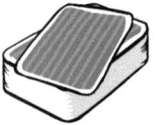

deck of cards
لعبة الورق

jigsaw
أحجية

SUPER
MEGA

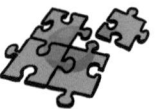

comic
رسوم هزلية

lego bricks

أحجار الليغو

toy blocks

حجارة تركيب

action figure

دمية بطل

romper suit

لباس الطفل

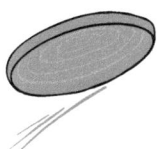

frisbee

فريسبي

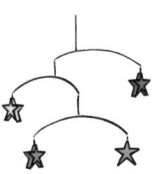

mobile

دمية معلقة

board game

لعبة الطاولة

dice

لعبة النرد

model train set

لعبة قطار

pacifier

مصاصة

party

حفلة

picture book

كتاب مصوّر

ball

كرة

doll

دمية

play

يلعب

sandpit

ملعب رملي للأطفال

swing

أرجوحة

toys

لعبة

video game console

ألعاب فيديو

tricycle

دراجة ثلاثية

teddy bear

دمية على شكل الدب

wardrobe

خزانة الثياب

clothing

ثياب

socks

جوارب قصيرة

stockings

جوارب طويلة

tights

جورب بنطلون

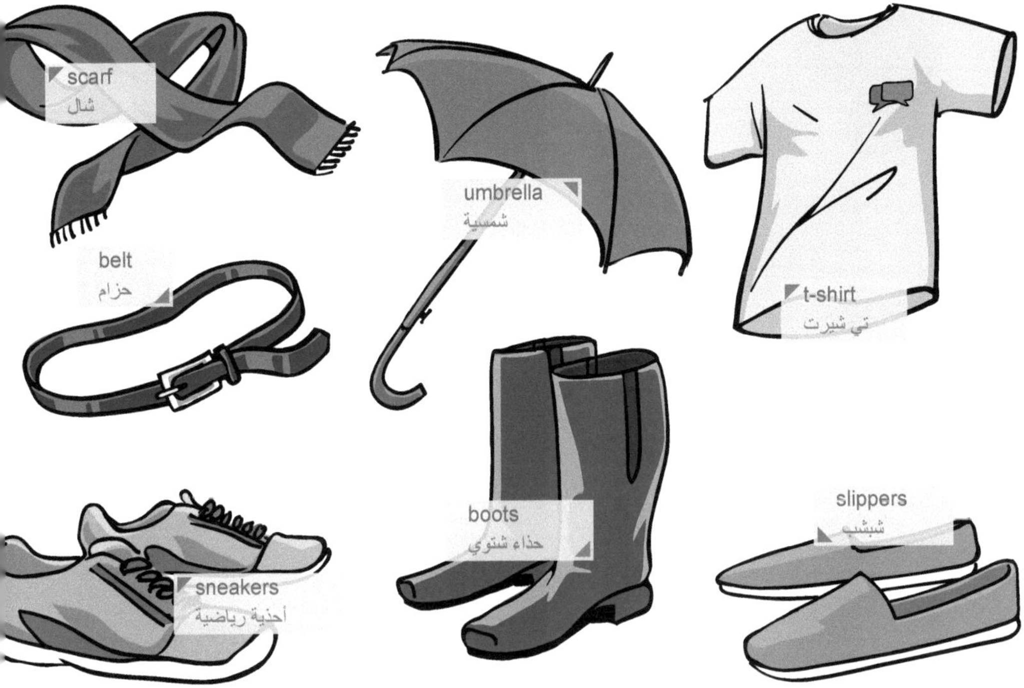

scarf
شال

umbrella
شمسية

t-shirt
تي شيرت

belt
حزام

boots
حذاء شتوي

slippers
شبشب

sneakers
أحذية رياضية

sandals
....
صندل

shoes
....
حذاء

rubber boots
....
جزمة كاوتشوك

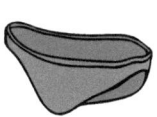

underwear
....
سروال داخلي

bra
....
صدّارة

undershirt
....
قميص داخلي

body

لباس ملاصق للجسم

pants

بنطلون

jeans

جينز

skirt

تنورة

blouse

بلوزة

shirt

قميص

pullover

سترة قطنية

sweater

كنزة كم طويل

blazer

سترة فضفاضة

jacket

سترة

coat

معطف

raincoat

معطف مطري

costume

زي - طقم نسائي

dress

ثوب

wedding dress

ثوب الزفاف

suit

طقم

nightgown

قميص نوم

pajamas

بيجاما

sari

ساري

headscarf

حجاب

turban

عمامة

burka

برقع

kaftan

قفطان

abaya

عباءة

swimsuit

مايوه

trunks

سروال سباحة

shorts

شرت

tracksuit

بدلة رياضية

apron

مئزر

gloves

قفازات

button

زر

glasses

نظارة

bracelet

إسوارة

necklace

عقْد

ring

خاتم

earring

قرط

cap

طاقيّة

coat hanger

علاقة ثياب

hat

قبّعة

tie

ربطة العنق

zip

سحّاب

helmet

خوذة

braces

حمّالة البنطلون

school uniform

اللباس المدرسي

uniform

زي موحّد

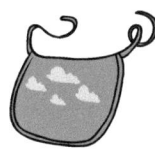

bib

مريلة الأطفال

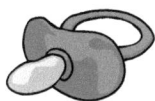

pacifier

مصّاصة

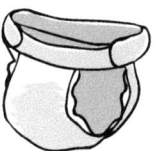

diaper

لفافة

office

مكتب

server
المخدّم
filing cabinet
خزانة الملفات
printer
طابعة
paper
ورقة
monitor
شاشة
mouse
فارة
desk
طاولة المكتب
folder
ملف
keyboard
لوحة المفاتيح
waste-paper basket
قمامة
computer
حاسوب
chair
كرسي

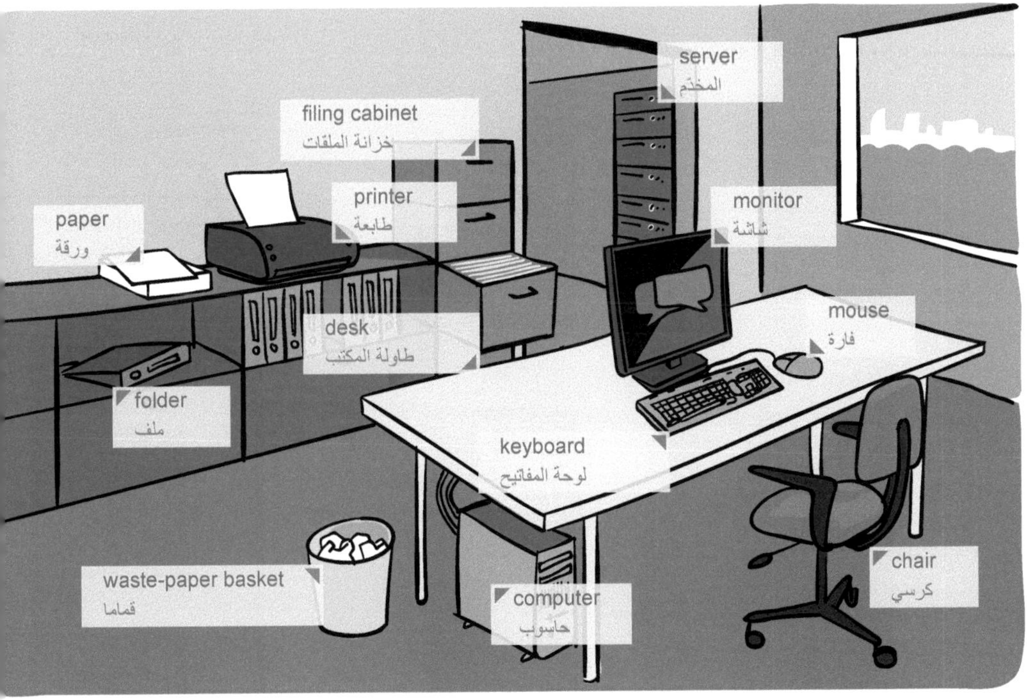

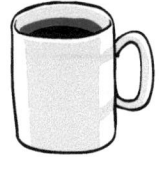

coffee mug

كأس من القهوة

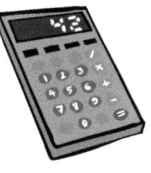

calculator

الآلة الحاسبة

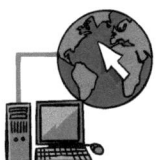

internet

الإنترنت

laptop

الحاسوب المحمول

letter

رسالة

message

خبر

cell phone

الهاتف المحمول

network

شبكة

photocopier

جهاز تصوير

software

البرمجيات

telephone

هاتف

plug socket

مقبس كهربائي

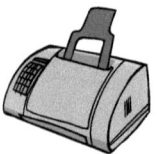

fax machine

فاكس

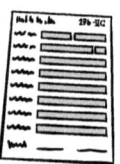

form

استمارة

document

وثيقة

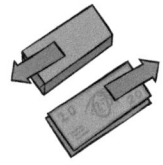

buy

يشتري

pay

يدفع

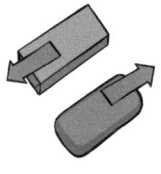

trade

يتاجر

money

مال

dollar

دولار

euro

يورو

yen

ين

rouble

روبل

Swiss franc

فرنك سويسري

renminbi yuan

يوان

rupee

روبية

cash point

صرّاف آلي

currency exchange office

مكتب صرافة

gold

ذهب

silver

فضة

oil

نفط

energy

طاقة

price

سعر

contract

عقد

tax

ضريبة

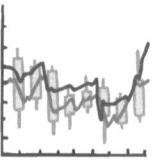

stock

سهم

work

يعمل

employee

موظف

employer

رب العمل

factory

مصنع

shop

متجر

occupations

المِهَن

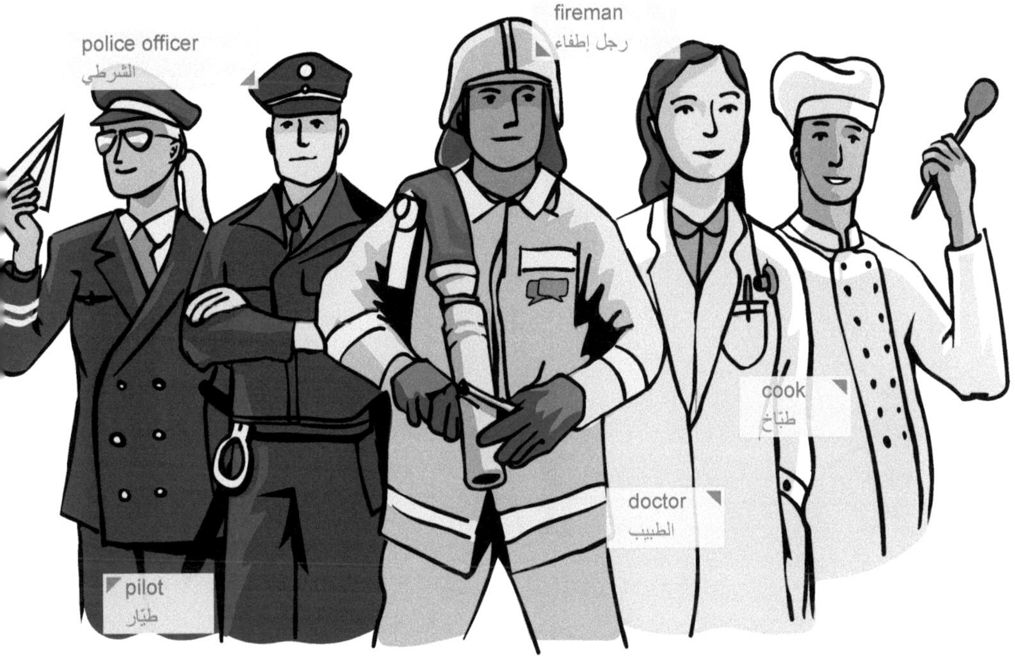

police officer
الشرطي
fireman
رجل إطفاء
cook
طبّاخ
doctor
الطبيب
pilot
طيّار

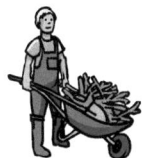

gardener

بستاني

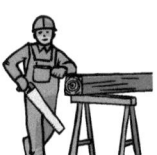

carpenter

نجّار

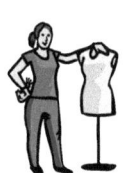

seamstress

خيّاطة

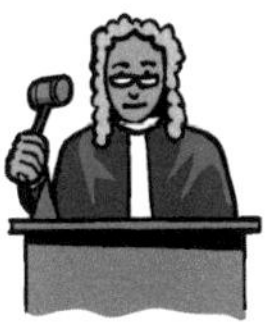

judge

قاض

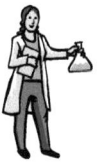

chemist

كيميائي

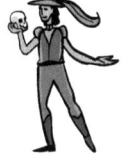

actor

ممثل

bus driver

سائق حافلة

taxi driver

سائق تاكسي

fisherman

صياد سمك

cleaning lady

أجيرة للتنظيف

roofer

بنّاء سقف

waiter

نادل

hunter

صيّاد

painter

رسّام

baker

خباز

electrician

كهربائي

builder

عامل بناء

engineer

مهندس

butcher

لحّام

plumber

سمكري

postman

ساعي البريد

soldier

جندي

architect

مهندس معماري

cashier

أمين صندوق

florist

بائع الزهور

hairdresser

حلاق

conductor

مراقب القطار

mechanic

ميكانيكي

captain

قبطان

dentist

طبيب أسنان

scientist

رجل العلم

rabbi

حاخام

imam

إمام

monk

راهب

pastor

كاهن

occupations - المِهَن

tools

عدة عمل

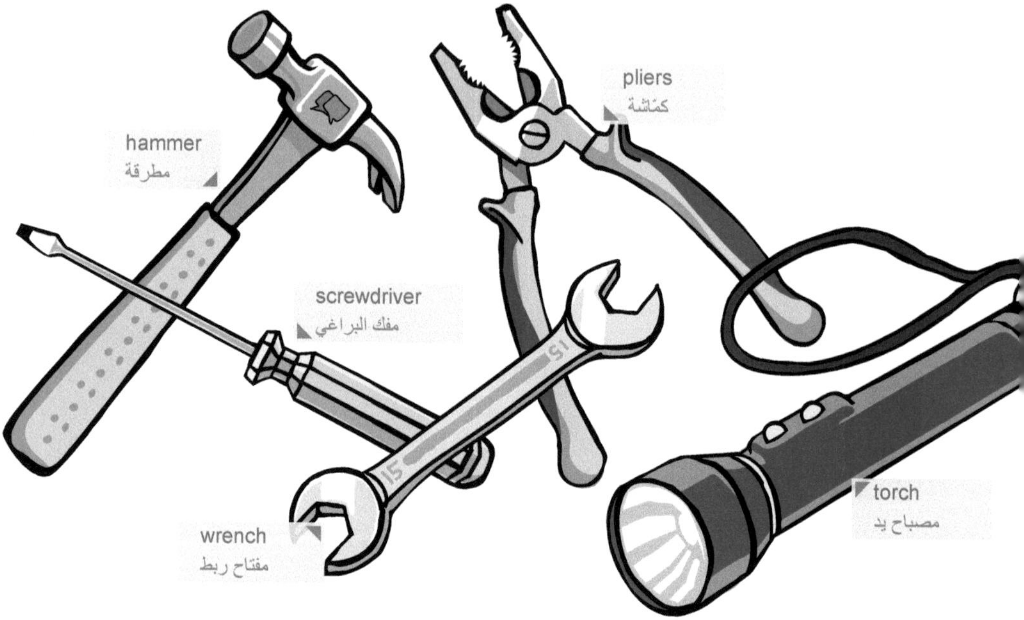
hammer
مطرقة
pliers
كمّاشة
screwdriver
مفك البراغي
wrench
مفتاح ربط
torch
مصباح يد

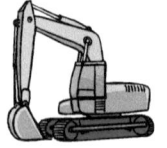

excavator
جرافة

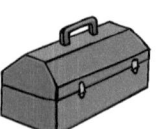

toolbox
صندوق العدة

ladder
سلّم

saw
منشار

nails
مسامير

drill
مثقب

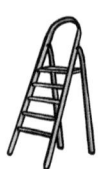

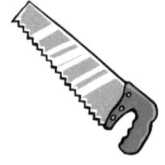

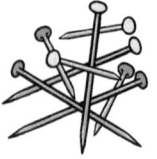

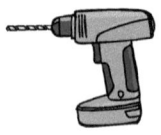

repair

يصلح

shovel

مجرفة

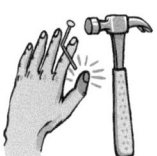

Damn!

اللعنة

dustpan

لقاطة الكناسة

paint can

سطل الألوان

screws

براغي

musical instruments

آلات موسيقية

loud speaker
مكبر الصوت

drum set
آلات الإيقاع

guitar
غيتار

double bass
كمان أجهر

trumpet
بوق

piano

بيانو

violin

كمنجة

bass

جهير

timpani

طبل كبير

drums

طبل

keyboard

بيانو كهربائي

saxophone

ساكسوفون

flute

ناي

microphone

ميكروفون

ZOO
حديقة حيوانات

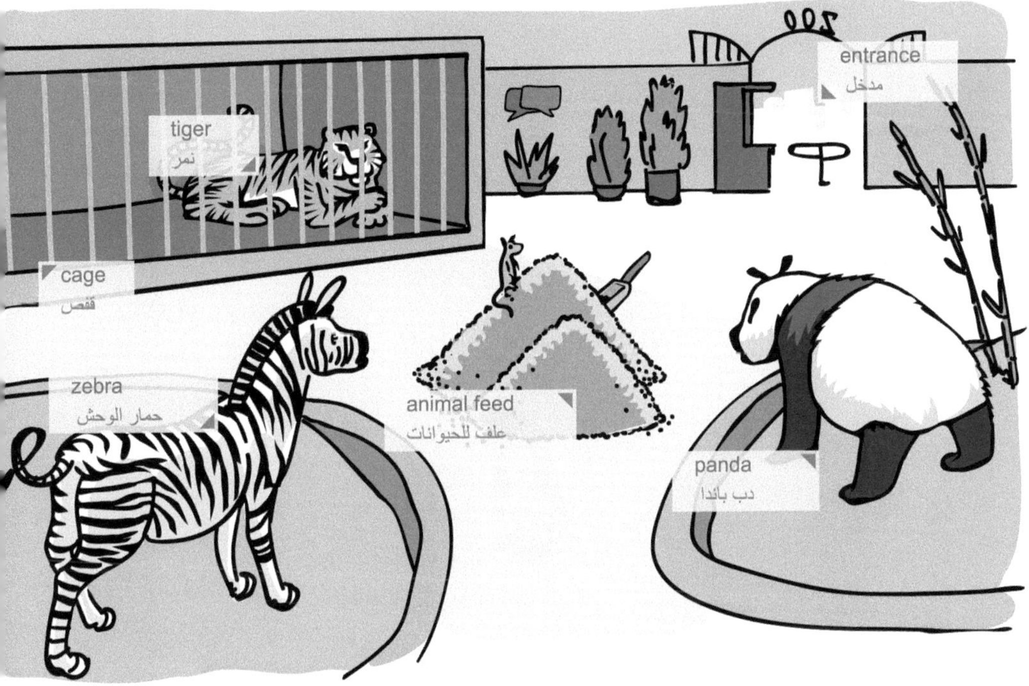
entrance
مدخل
tiger
نمر
cage
قفص
zebra
حمار الوحش
animal feed
علف للحيوانات
panda
دب باندا

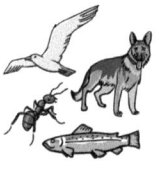

animals
حيوانات

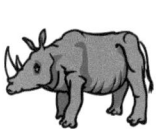

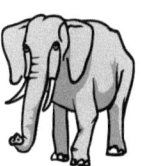

elephant
فيل

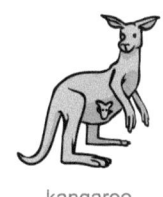

kangaroo
كنغر

rhino
وحيد القرن

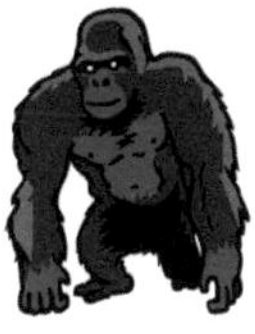

gorilla
غوريلا

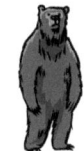

bear
دب

camel

جمل

ostrich

نعامة

lion

أسد

monkey

قرد

flamingo

طائر فلامينغو

parrot

ببغاء

polar bear

دب قطبي

penguin

بطريق

shark

سمك القرش

peacock

طاووس

snake

أفعى

crocodile

تمساح

zookeeper

حارس في حديقة الحيوان

seal

عجل البحر

jaguar

نمر أمريكي مرقط

pony

فرس قزم

leopard

نمر

hippo

فرس النهر

giraffe

زرافة

eagle

نسر

boar

خنزير برّي

fish

سمك

turtle

سلحفاة

walrus

حيوان فظ البحري

fox

ثعلب

gazelle

غزال

American football
كرة القدم الأمريكية

cycling
ركوب الدراجات

tennis
كرة التنس

basketball
كرة السلة

swimming
السباحة

boxing
الملاكمة

ice hockey
هوكي الجليد

soccer

كرة القدم

badminton

الريشة الطائرة

athletics

ألعاب القوى الخفيفة

handball

كرة اليد

skiing

التزلج على الثلج

polo

بولو

jump
يقفز

laugh
يضحك

hug
يعانق

walk
يمشي

sing
يغني

dream
يحلم

pray
يصلي

kiss
يقبّل

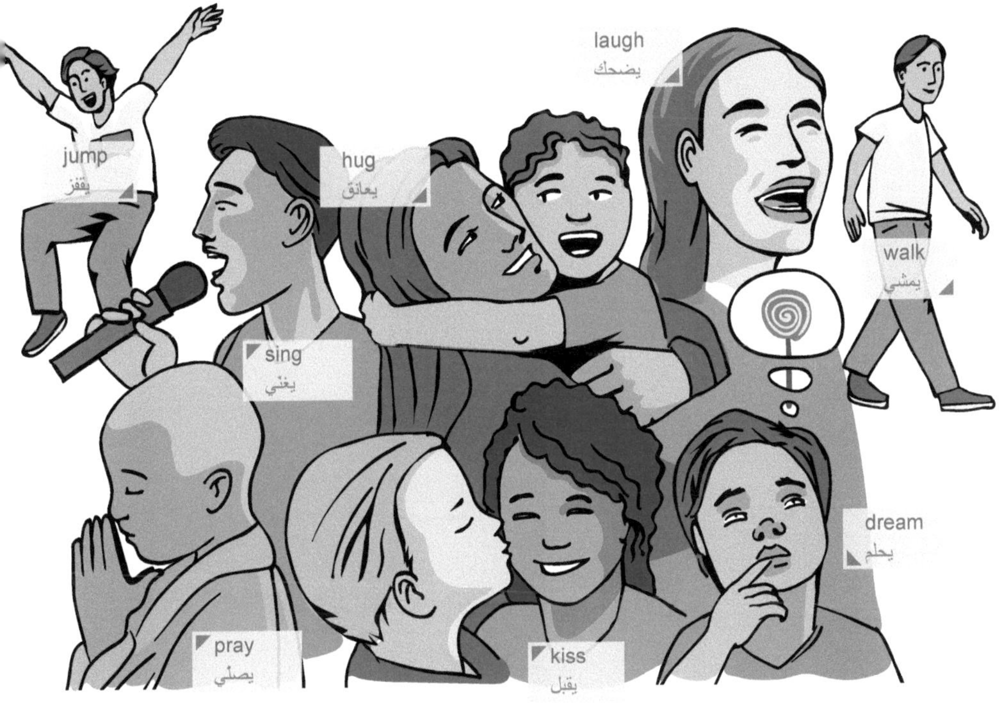

write

يكتب

draw

يرسم

show

يُري

push

يدفع

give

يعطي

take

يأخذ

have

يملك

do

يعمل

be

يوجد

stand

يَقِف

run

يركض

pull

يسحب

throw

يرمي

fall

يقع

lie

يستلقي

wait

ينتظر

carry

يحمل

sit

يجلس

get dressed

يلبس

sleep

ينام

wake up

يستيقظ

look at

ينظر إلى ..

cry

يبكي

stroke

يمسّد

comb

يمشّط

talk

يتكلم

understand

يفهم

ask

يسأل

listen

يسمع

drink

يشرب

eat

يأكل

tidy up

يرتّب

love

يحب

cook

يطبخ

drive

يقود

fly

يطير

sail

يبحر بزورق شراعي

calculate

يحسب

read

يقرأ

learn

يتعلم

work

يعمل

marry

يتزوج

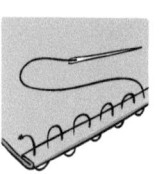

sew

يخيط

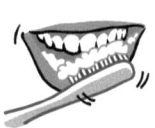

brush teeth

ينظف أسنانه

kill

يقتل

smoke

يدخّن

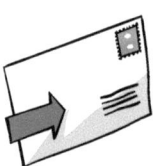

send

يرسل

family
عائلة

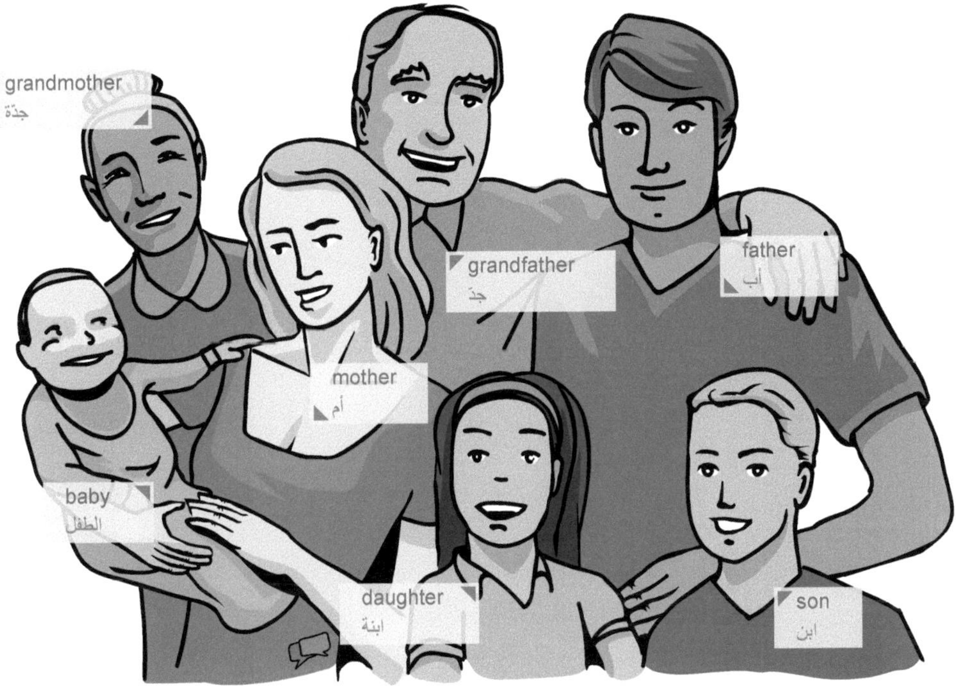
grandmother
جدّة
grandfather
جدّ
father
أب
mother
أم
baby
الطفل
daughter
ابنة
son
ابن

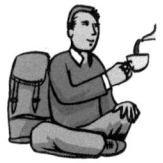

guest
ضيف

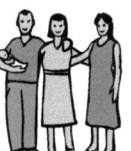

aunt
عمّة / خالة

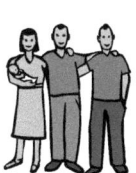

uncle
عمّ / خال

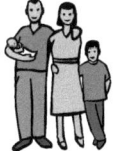

brother
أخ

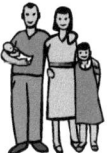

sister
أخت

body

الجسم

forehead
الجبين
eye
العين
face
الوجه
chin
الذقن
breast
الصدر
finger
الإصبع
hand
اليد
arm
الذراع
shoulder
الكتف
leg
الساق

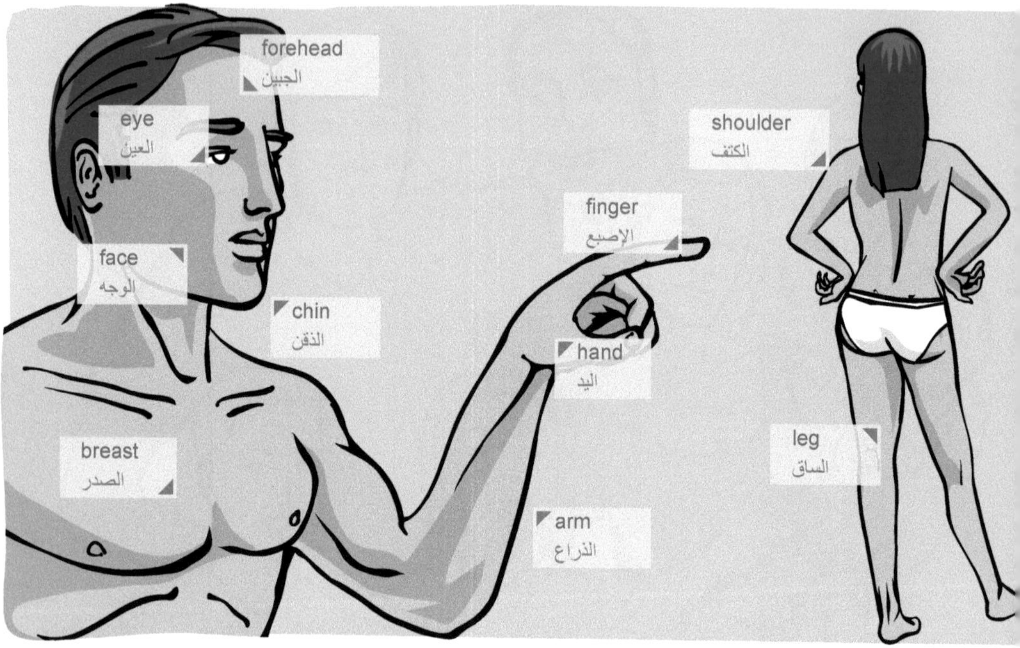

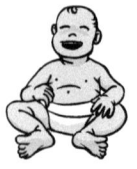

baby

الطفل

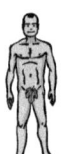

man

الرجل

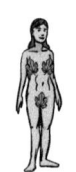

woman

المرأة

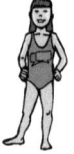

girl

البنت

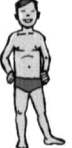

boy

الولد

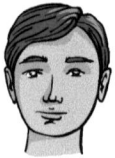

head

الرأس

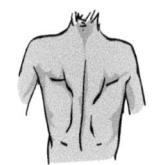

back

الظهر

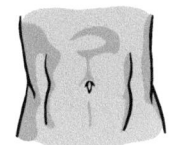

belly

البطن

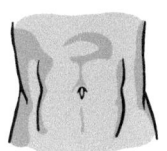

navel

السرّة

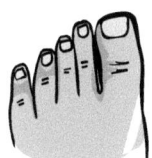

toe

إصبع القدم

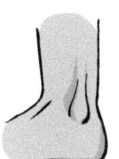

heel

الكعب

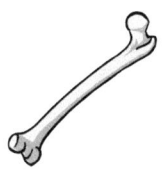

bone

العظم

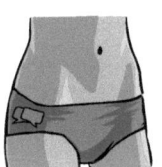

hip

الورك

knee

الركبة

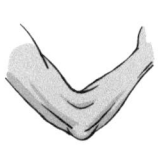

elbow

المرفق

nose

الأنف

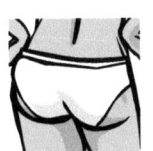

buttocks

العَجُز

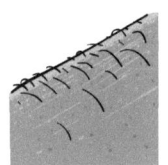

skin

البَشرة

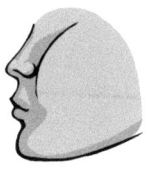

cheek

الخد

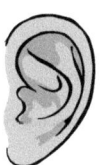

ear

الأذن

lip

الشفة

mouth

الفم

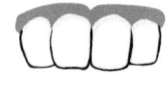

tooth

السن

tongue

اللسان

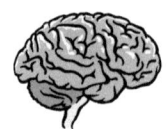

brain

الدماغ

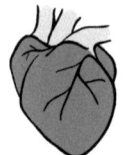

heart

القلب

muscle

العضلة

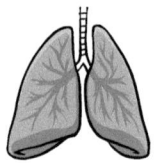

lung

الرئة

liver

الكبد

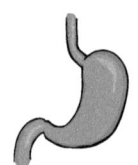

stomach

المعدة

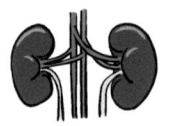

kidneys

الكلى

sex

الاتصال الجنسي

condom

الواقي المطاطي

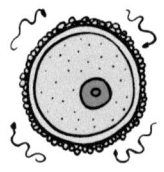

ovum

البويضة

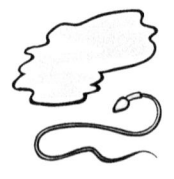

semen

المنيّ

pregnancy

الحمل

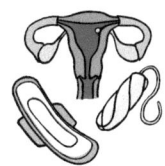

menstruation

الحيض

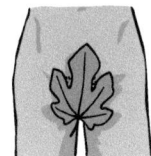

vagina

المهبل

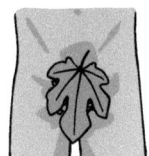

penis

القضيب

eyebrow

الحاجب

hair

الشعر

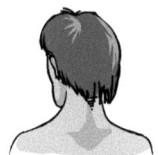

neck

الرقبة

hospital
المستشفى

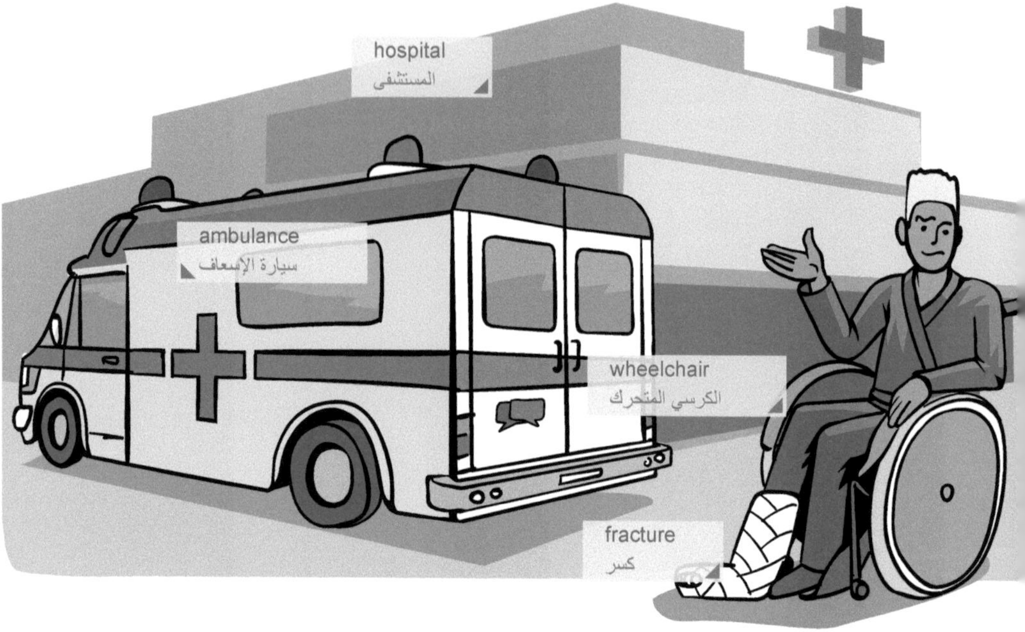

hospital
المستشفى
ambulance
سيارة الإسعاف
wheelchair
الكرسي المتحرك
fracture
كسر

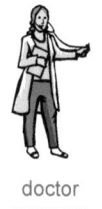

doctor
الطبيب

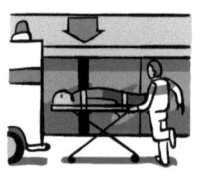

emergency room
غرفة الإسعاف

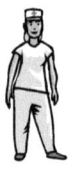

nurse
الممرضة

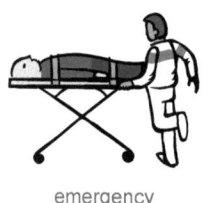

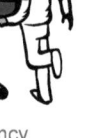

emergency
حالة

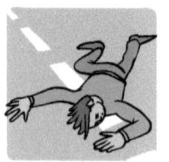

unconscious
مغمى عليه

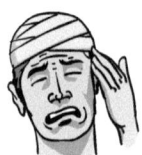

pain
الألم

injury

إصابة

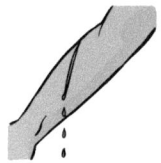

bleeding

النزيف

heart attack

احتشاء القلب

stroke

جلطة

allergy

حسسية

cough

السعال

fever

الحُمّى

flu

إنفلونزا

diarrhea

الإسهال

headache

وجع الرأس

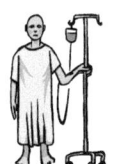

cancer

السرطان

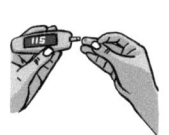

diabetes

مرض السكر

surgeon

جرّاح

scalpel

مبضع

operation

عملية

CT

سيتي سكان

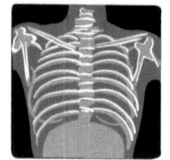

x-ray

الأشعة السينية

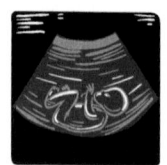

ultrasound

فوق الصوتي

face mask

القناع

disease

المرض

waiting room

غرفة الانتظار

crutch

العُكّاز

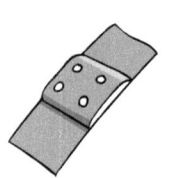

plaster

شريط لاصق

bandage

ضماد

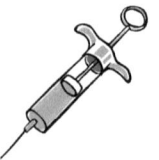

injection

حقنة

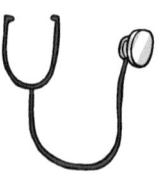

stethoscope

سمّاعة الطبيب

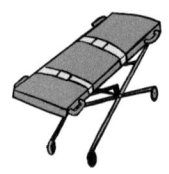

stretcher

نقالة

clinical thermometer

ميزان حرارة

birth

ولادة

overweight

وزن زائد

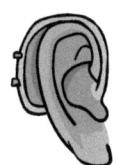

hearing aid

جهاز السمع

disinfectant

المواد المعقمة

infection

عدوى

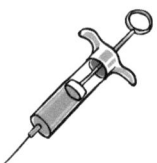

virus

فيروس

HIV / AIDS

الإيدز

medicine

الطب

vaccination

اللقاح

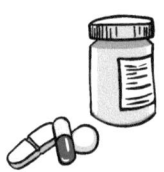

tablets

أقراص الدواء

pill

حبّة الدواء

emergency call

نداء النجدة

blood pressure monitor

مقياس ضغط الدم

ill / healthy

مريض / صحيح

Help!

النجدة!

alarm

إنذار

assault

اعتداء

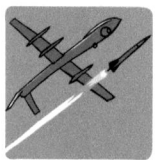

attack

هجوم

danger

خطر

emergency exit

مخرج طوارئ

Fire!

حريق!

fire extinguisher

جهاز الإطفاء

accident

حادث

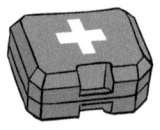

first-aid kit

حقيبة الإسعاف الأولى

SOS

أنقذونا

police

الشرطة

Europe

أوروبا

North America

أمريكا الشمالية

South America

أمريكا الجنوبية

Africa

أفريقيا

Asia

آسيا

Australia

أستراليا

Atlantic

المحيط الأطلسي

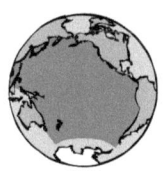

Pacific

المحيط الهادي

Indian Ocean

المحيط الهندي

Antarctic Ocean

المحيط المتجمد الجنوبي

Arctic Ocean

المحيط المتجمد الشمالي

North pole

القطب الشمالي

South pole

القطب الجنوبي

Antarctica

منطقة القطب الجنوبي

earth

أرض

land

بر

sea

بحر

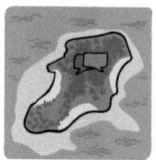

island

جزيرة

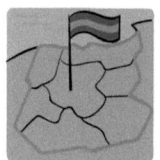

nation

أمة

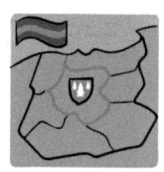

state

دولة

clock face

ميناء الساعة

hour hand

عقرب الساعات

minute hand

عقرب الدقائق

second hand

عقرب الثواني

What time is it?

كم الساعة الآن؟

day

يوم

time

زمن

now

الآن

digital watch

ساعة رقمية

minute

دقيقة

hour

ساعة

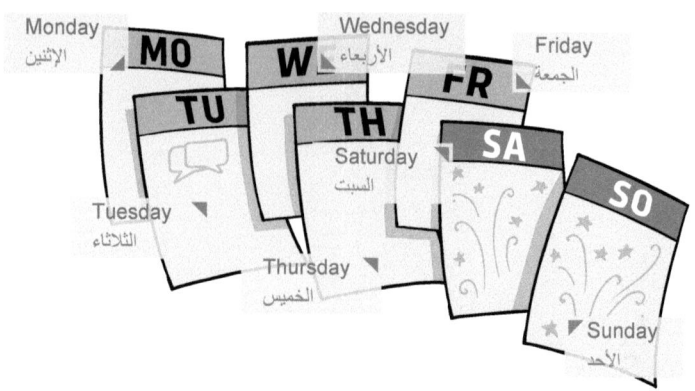

Monday — الإثنين
Wednesday — الأربعاء
Friday — الجمعة
Tuesday — الثلاثاء
Saturday — السبت
Thursday — الخميس
Sunday — الأحد

yesterday

الأمس

today

اليوم

tomorrow

غدا

morning

الصباح

noon

الظهر

evening

المساء

workdays

أيام العمل

weekend

نهاية الأسبوع

rain
مطر

snow
ثلج

wind
ريح

spring
الربيع

fall
الخريف

summer
الصيف

winter
الشتاء

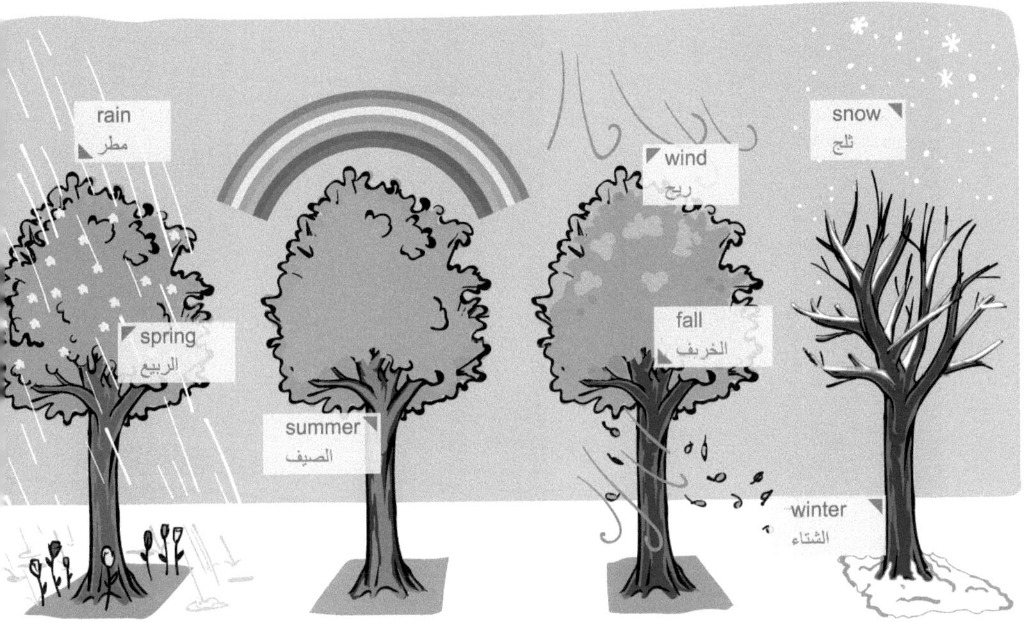

weather forecast

التنبّؤ بالحالة الجوية

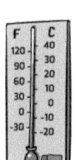

thermometer

مقياس حرارة

sunshine

ضوء الشمس

cloud

سحابة

fog

ضباب

humidity

رطوبة الجو

lightning

برق

thunder

رعد

storm

عاصفة

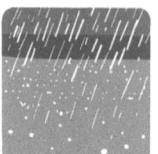

hail

بَرَد

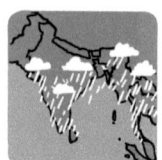

monsoon

ريح موسمية

flood

طوفان

ice

جليد

January

كانون الثاني / يناير

February

شباط / فبراير

March

آذار / مارس

April

نيسان / أبريل

May

أيار / مايو

June

حزيران / يونيو

July

تموز / يوليو

August

أب / أغسطس

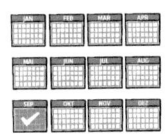

September
....
أيلول / سبتمبر

October
....
تشرين الأول / أكتوبر

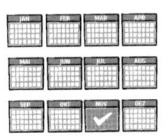

November
....
تشرين الثاني / نوفمبر

December
....
كانون الأول / ديسمبر

shapes

أشكال

circle
....
دائرة

square
....
مربّع

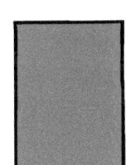

rectangle
....
مستطيل

triangle
....
مثلّث

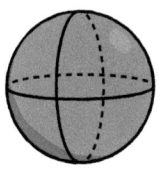

sphere
....
كرة

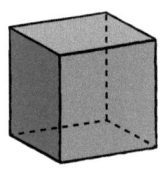

cube
....
مكعب

colors

ألوان

white

أبيض

yellow

أصفر

orange

برتقالي

pink

وردي

red

أحمر

purple

بنفسجي

blue

أزرق

green

أخضر

brown

بني

gray

رمادي

black

أسود

a lot / a little

كثير / قليل

angry / calm

غضبان / هادئ

beautiful / ugly

جميل / قبيح

beginning / end

بداية / نهاية

big / small

كبير / صغير

bright / dark

فاتح / قاتم

brother / sister

أخ / أخت

clean / dirty

نظيف / وسخ

complete / incomplete

كامل / ناقص

day / night

نهار / ليل

dead / alive

ميت / حيّ

wide / narrow

عريض / ضيّق

edible / inedible

صالح للأكل / غير صالح

evil / kind

شرّير / لطيف

excited / bored

مثير / ممل

fat / thin

سمين / نحيف

first / last

أولا / أخيرا

friend / enemy

صديق / عدو

full / empty

مليء / فارغ

hard / soft

صلب / ليّن

heavy / light

ثقيل / خفيف

hunger / thirst

جوع / عطش

ill / healthy

مريض / صحيح

illegal / legal

غير شرعي / شرعي

intelligent / stupid

ذكي / غبي

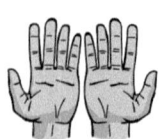

left / right

يسار / يمين

near / far

قريب / بعيد

new / used

جديد / مستعمل

nothing / something

لا شيء / بعض الشيء

old / young

مسن / شاب

on / off

يشعل / يطفئ

open / closed

مفتوح / مغلق

quiet / loud

خافت / عالٍ

rich / poor

غني / فقير

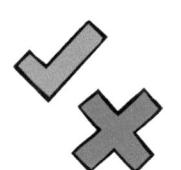

right / wrong

صح / خطأ

rough / smooth

أخرش / أملس

sad / happy

حزين / سعيد

short / long

قصير / طويل

slow / fast

بطيء / سريع

wet / dry

مبلول / جاف

warm / cool

ساخن / بارد

war / peace

حرب / سلم

0	**1**	**2**
zero	one	two
صفر	واحد	اثنان

3	**4**	**5**
three	four	five
ثلاثة	أربعة	خمسة

6	**7**	**8**
six	seven	eight
ستة	سبعة	ثمانية

9	**10**	**11**
nine	ten	eleven
تسعة	عشرة	أحد عشر

12

twelve

اثنا عشر

13

thirteen

ثلاثة عشر

14

fourteen

أربعة عشر

15

fifteen

خمسة عشر

16

sixteen

ستة عشر

17

seventeen

سبعة عشر

18

eighteen

ثمانية عشر

19

nineteen

تسعة عشر

20

twenty

عشرون

100

hundred

مائة

1.000

thousand

ألف

1.000.000

million

مليون

English

الإنكليزية

American English

الإنكليزية الأمريكية

Chinese Mandarin

لغة ماندارين الصينية

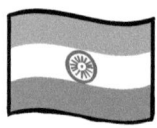

Hindi

الهندية

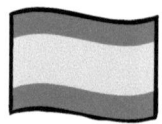

Spanish

الإسبانية

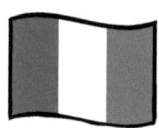

French

الفرنسية

Arabic

العربية

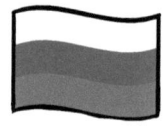

Russian

الروسية

Portuguese

البرتغالية

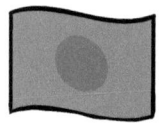

Bengali

البنغالية

German

الألمانية

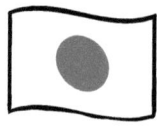

Japanese

اليابانية

I

أنا

you

أنت

he / she / it

هو / هي

we

نحن

you

أنتم

they

هم

who?

من؟

what?

ماذا؟

how?

كيف؟

where?

أين؟

when?

متى؟

name

اسم

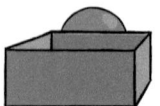

behind

خلف

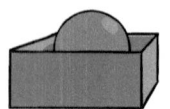

in

في

in front of

أمام

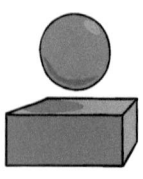

over

فوق

on

على

under

تحت

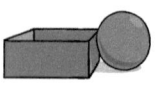

beside

جنب

between

بين

place

مكان